THIS LITTLE

LAP SONGS, FINGER PLAYS,
CLAPPING GAMES AND ACTION RHYMES

WALKER BOOKS
AND SUBSIDIARIES
LONDON · BOSTON · SYDNEY · AUCKLAND

PIGGY

AND OTHER RHYMES TO SING AND PLAY

EDITED BY JANE YOLEN

ILLUSTRATED BY WILL HILLENBRAND

MUSICAL ARRANGEMENTS BY ADAM STEMPLE

Peek-a-boo to my newest grandchildren,

the twins Caroline and Amelia

J. Y.

◆

To Denise Fleming and David, I love you both!

With special thanks to Chris, Liz and Heather,

my dream team!

W. H.

◆

For wee David and lovely Alison,

the best audience these songs have ever had

A. S.

◆

First published 2005 by Walker Books Ltd

87 Vauxhall Walk, London SE11 5HJ

2 4 6 8 10 9 7 5 3 1

Collection and introduction © 2005 Jane Yolen

Illustrations © 2005 Will Hillenbrand

Musical arrangements © 2005 Adam Stemple

Musical arrangements (UK publication) "Dance to Your Daddy", "Ride a Cock-Horse",

"See-Saw, Margery Daw", "The Grand Old Duke of York", "Hickory, Dickory Dock"

and "I'm a Little Teapot" © 2005 Barry Gibson

"Down By the Station" by Lee Ricks and Slim Galliard © 1948 (renewed 1976) EMI Mills Music Inc. All rights

reserved. Used by permission Warner Brothers Publications U.S. Inc., Miami, Florida 33014

This book has been typeset in Mrs. Eaves

Printed in China

British Library Cataloguing in Publication Data:

a catalogue record for this book is available from the British Library

ISBN 1-4063-0044-6

www.walkerbooks.co.uk

Peek-a-boo
An Introduction

Peek-a-boo is that classic baby game, probably the most easily recognized throughout the world. To play, you simply cover and uncover your face with your hands and say to the toddler:

Peek-a-boo,
I see you!

or possibly:
Peek-a-boo,
Mummy (Daddy) sees you!

or even:
Where's the baby?
Peek-a-boo!
There's the baby — I see you!

I have played this with my own children and grandchildren. I have played it with children on buses, across the aisles on aeroplanes, in audiences when a desperate mother was trying to calm a baby, and even at a funeral when a fussy infant threatened to undo us all.

None of the lap games in this book are difficult. But they unite us across borders, across ages and across abilities.

Even before a child can talk, can walk, can name the parts of the body, play is essential. The lap is a kind of schoolroom. What a child learns there is learned forever.

Peek-a-boo.
I love you.

Jane Yolen
2005

CONTENTS

CLAP, CLAP, CLAP

TAKE A BOW

Up and

Down

DANCE TO YOUR DADDY

This rhyme was popular in the eighteenth and nineteenth centuries, particularly in Scotland and the north of England. The word lady *may be substituted for* laddie.

Bouncily

Dance to your dad-dy, My lit-tle lad-die, Dance to your dad-dy,

My_ lit-tle lamb! You shall have a fish-y On a lit-tle dish-y,

You shall have a had-dock When the boat comes in.

Dance to your daddy,

My little laddie,

Dance to your daddy,

My little lamb!

You shall have an apple,

You shall have a plum,

You shall have an apple

When your dad comes home.

To play: The dance starts on the lap and then soars into the air.
For "apple" and "plum", lift the child up to pick the fruit from imaginary trees.

DANCE, LITTLE BABY

A popular rhyme from the nineteenth century.
To crow *is to make a gleeful sound.* Caper *is the old word for play.*
Coral *is a nineteenth century word for a rattle ornamented with a bit of coral.*

Dance, little baby, dance up high,

Never mind, baby, Mother is by.

Crow and caper, caper and crow,

There, little baby, down you go.

Up to the ceiling, down to the ground,

Backwards and forwards, round and round.

Dance, little baby, and Mother shall sing,

With the merry gay coral, ding, ding-a-ding, ding.

To play: Lift the baby up and over your head,
then down to your lap, according to the words of the rhyme.

Up the Wooden Hill

A bedtime rhyme that begins
with a lift and ends with a blanket.

Up the wooden hill

To Bedfordshire,

Down Sheet Lane

To Blanket Fair.

To play: Lift the child up the wooden hill (the stairs,
if you have them) and swoop down into bed.

CATCH HIM, CROW

This lift-and-lower rhyme is an ancestor of "Rock-a-bye, Baby".

Catch him, crow, carry him, kite!

Take him away till the apples are ripe.

When they are ripe and ready to fall,

Here comes baby, apples, and all.

**To play: Lift the baby high, then higher, and
then — with a playful swoop — let the baby
down to your lap again.**

UP IN THE GREEN ORCHARD

This rhyme originated in the nineteenth century.

Up in the green orchard

there is a green tree,

The finest of pippins that ever you see.

The apples are ripe,

and ready to fall,

And Reuben and Robin

shall gather them all!

**To play: Lift the baby up as if gathering the apples.
You may substitute your baby's name and
your own for Reuben and Robin.**

How Many Days?

This little rhyme first appeared in Thomas Fleet's Songs for the Nursery, *in the eighteenth century.*
If the lap is baby's classroom, here is one of the earliest lessons.

How many days has my baby to play?

Saturday, Sunday, Monday,

Tuesday, Wednesday, Thursday, Friday,

Saturday, Sunday, Monday.

Hop away, skip away,

My baby wants to play.

My baby wants to play every day.

To play: Lift the child for each day of the week, as well as on the "hop"
and "skip" line. Settle back down in your lap for the final line.

Originally a rhyme called "Old Father Long-Legs" about
daddy longlegs, this verse has migrated into a rhyme about a goose.
According to some scholars, it is actually a political rhyme about Cardinal Beaton,
who was assassinated in 1546 because of a dispute over prayer books.

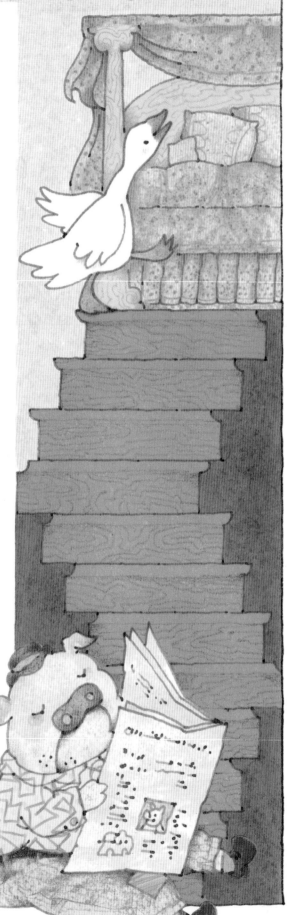

Goosey, goosey, gander

Whither shall I wander?

Upstairs and downstairs

And in my lady's chamber.

There I met an old man

Who would not say his prayers.

I took him by the left leg

And threw him down the stairs.

To play: Start with the child on your lap, but lift the child to
wander up and down and back into your lap for the lady's chamber. Do not
actually lift the child by the left leg or throw them down the stairs!

There Was an Old Woman

The oldest print version of this can be found in John Newbery's Mother Goose's Melody, *first published in 1760.*

There was an old woman tossed up in a blanket

Seventeen times as high as the moon;

Where she was going I couldn't but ask it,

For in her hand she carried a broom.

Old woman, old woman, old woman, quoth I,

Where are you going to up so high?

To brush the cobwebs off the sky!

May I go with you?

Ay, by-and-by.

To play: This is a tossing-in-the-air game, though if, like me, you are
afraid of doing such a thing, keep hold of the child all the time.

Bumpety,

Bumpety

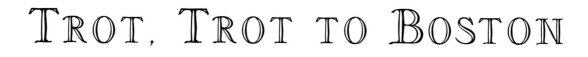

TROT, TROT TO BOSTON

Boston, Lynn, Dover and Lyme are both American and English towns,
but this is usually considered an American lap game.

Trot, trot to Boston,

Trot, trot to Lynn,

Look out, Baby,

You're going to fall in!

Trot, trot to Boston,

Trot, trot to Dover,

Look out, Baby,

You're going to turn over!

Trot, trot to Boston,

Trot, trot to Lyme,

Look out, Baby,

We'll bounce another time!

To play: Sit the child on your lap, facing you, and bounce the child up and down.
Substitute your own child's name for "Baby". On the final word, open your legs and
the child will slip through. Of course, keep a good grip on the child's hands!

This Is the Way the Farmer Rides

This knee-trotting song is closely related to the old nursery rhyme "This Is the Way the Ladies Ride".

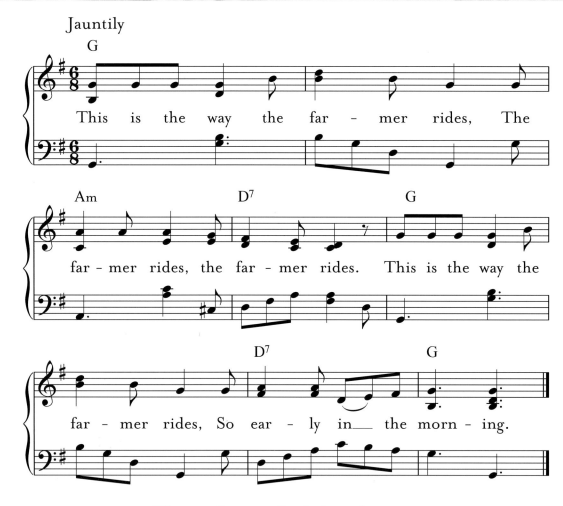

This is the way the lady rides, etc.

This is the way the gentleman rides, etc.

This is the way that Baby rides, etc.

To play: The child sits facing you on your knees (or in some versions, on your crossed legs). Bounce the child in rhythm: with vigour for the farmer, daintily for the lady, jauntily for the gentleman and then with great joy for the child. But please remember to hold on to the child's hands firmly the whole time!

A Farmer Went Trotting

In the early nineteenth century, this was a popular nursery rhyme. It became even more popular when in 1884 the illustrator Randolph Caldecott made a picture book with the verse as his text.

A farmer went trotting upon his grey mare,

Bumpety, bumpety, bump.

With his daughter behind him so rosy and fair,

Lumpety, lumpety, lump.

A raven cried, "Croak!" And they all tumbled down,

Bumpety, bumpety, bump.

The mare broke her knees and the farmer his crown,

Lumpety, lumpety, lump.

This mischievous raven flew laughing away,

Bumpety, bumpety, bump.

And vowed he would serve them the same the next day,

Lumpety, lumpety, lump!

To play: A great knee-bouncer this, with its "tumble down" in the middle of the rhyme and not the end.

HERE GOES MY LORD

An alternative version to
"This Is the Way the Farmer Rides".

Here goes my lord,

A trot! A trot! A trot! A trot!

Here goes my lady,

A canter! A canter! A canter! A canter!

Here goes my young master,

Jockey-hitch! Jockey-hitch! Jockey-hitch!

Jockey-hitch!

Here goes my young miss,

An amble! An amble! An amble! An amble!

The footman lags behind to tipple ale and wine,

And goes gallop, a gallop, a gallop to make

up his time.

To play: The child sits on your knee, facing you, and is bounced in rhythm.

A GENTLEMAN OF WALES

This rhyme mixes references to Wales and Ireland with great abandon.
Pigtails in this instance refers to twists of tobacco.

Little John Morgan,

A gentleman of Wales,

Came riding on a nanny-goat

And selling of pigtails.

Chicky, cuckoo, my little duck,

See-saw, sickna downy;

Gallop a trot, gallop a trot,

And hey for Dublin towny!

To play: The child sits on your knee, facing you, and is bounced in rhythm.

Pray, Who Now Is Riding?

This translation of a Swedish knee-bouncing game can be found in a nineteenth century book of nursery rhymes.

And pray, who now is riding?
A lady it is that's riding.
And she goes with a gentle trot,
A gentle trot!

And pray, who now is riding?
A gentleman it is that's riding.
And he goes with a gallop-away,
A gallop-away!

And pray, who now is riding?
A farmer it is that's riding.
And he goes with a jog along,
A jog along!

To play: The child sits on your knee, facing you, and is bounced in rhythm.

Bell Horses

A nineteenth century knee-bouncing rhyme that was used for starting children's races.

Bell horses, bell horses,
What time of day?
One o'clock, two o'clock,
Three and away.

To play: Bounce the child according to the rhythm of the verse.

RIDE A COCK-HORSE

The words to this popular children's song go back at least as far as the 1600s and may have referred to Queen Elizabeth I or to Lady Godiva, or even to a lady of the day named Celia Fiennes, who rode throughout England in 1697.

A cock-horse is a child's rocking horse (or a parent's knee when it is being ridden).

Bouncily

Ride a cock-horse to Ban-bur-y Cross, To see a fine la-dy ride on a white horse. Rings on her fin-gers and bells on her toes, She shall have mu-sic wher-e-ver she goes.

To play: This begins as a regular knee-bouncer, at least for the first two lines. When the rings on the fingers are mentioned, kiss the child's hands one at a time. Then blow kisses to the child's feet for the bells on toes. Give a final knee bounce for the last line.

COVENTRY CROSS

There are several variants of "Ride a Cock-Horse" done without music,
but still clear cousins. Here is the most popular.

Ride a cock-horse to Coventry Cross,

To buy little Baby a galloping horse;

It trots on behind and it ambles before,

And Johnny can ride till he can ride no more.

Ride a cock-horse to Coventry Cross,

To see an old lady upon a black horse.

A ring on her finger, a bonnet of straw,

The strangest old lady that you ever saw.

To play: Bounce the child on the knee to the rhythm of the verse.

TO MARKET, TO MARKET

*Another knee-trotting rhyme, this one goes back to
a version from 1805 in* Songs for the Nursery.

To market, to market,

To buy a fat pig,

Home again, home again,

Jiggety-jig.

To market, to market,

To buy a fat hog,

Home again, home again,

Jiggety-jog.

To market, to market,

To buy a plum bun,

Home again, home again,

Marketing's done.

To play: With the child facing you, bounce your legs in time to the rhythm of the verse.

GEE UP, MY HORSE

In this knee-bouncing rhyme, the wonderful word elecampane refers to a kind of herbal sweet. Dobbin *is a popular old name for a horse.*

Gee up, my horse,

To Budleigh Fair.

What shall we have

When we get there?

Sugar and figs

And elecampane.

Home again, home again,

Master and Dame.

Gee up, my Dobbin,

And on to the fair.

What shall we buy

When we get there?

A penny an apple,

A penny a pear

Gee up, old Dobbin,

And off to the fair.

To play: Bounce the child on your knees to the rhythm of the verse.

See-Saw, Margery Daw

An actual see-saw — a wooden plank over a barrel — can be seen in the sixteenth century painter Brueghel's famous
Children's Games. *Such a game entered the English language sometime in the 1700s. But as a refrain the word*
was used much earlier, and probably referred to a two-handled saw. A daw *was a lazy or untidy woman.*

Gently rocking

See - saw, Mar - ge - ry Daw,

John - ny shall have a new mas - ter. He shall have but a

pen - ny a day Be - cause he can't work an - y fast - er.

To play: The child sits on your outstretched legs and is lifted and lowered in time to the music.

SEE-SAW, SACRADOWN

Sacradown is a word connected with sawyers, so this verse was clearly used with sawing before it was a children's game. Keep adding verses of your own.

See-saw, sacradown,

Which is the way to London town?

One foot up and the other foot down,

That is the way to London town.

See-saw, Jack in the hedge,

Which is the way to London Bridge?

One foot on the floor, one foot on the ledge,

That is the way to London Bridge.

See-saw, sacradown,

Which is the way to Boston town?

One foot up and the other foot down,

That is the way to Boston town.

To play: The child sits on your outstretched legs and gets a bumpy one-leg-up and one-leg-down ride.

THE GRAND OLD DUKE OF YORK

This Mother Goose rhyme actually refers to a historical personage:
Frederick Augustus, Duke of York, second son of King George III (1738—1820).
The hill mentioned is Mount Cassel in Belgium, which is featured in the
duke's unsuccessful campaign in Flanders.

To play: The child sits on your lap. Salute on the opening line. While bouncing the child in
rhythm and holding on with one hand, use your other hand to march your second and third
fingers up and over the child's tummy and chest, then touch the chin and march them down again!

Playful march

Oh the grand, old Duke of York, He had ten thou-sand men, He marched them up to the top of the hill, Then he marched them down a - gain.

And when they were up, they were up,

And when they were down, they were down.

And when they were only half-way up,

They were neither up nor down.

WIGGLE,

WIGGLE

THIS LITTLE PIGGY

This is probably one of the best-known toe-counters.

This little piggy went to market.

This little piggy stayed at home.

This little piggy ate roast beef.

This little piggy had none.

This little piggy cried,

"Wee, wee, wee,"

All the way home.

To play: Touch or hold on to the child's toes in succession, starting with the big toe. When you come to "Wee, wee, wee", let go of the toe and tickle the child, running up the leg to the tummy.

A PIGGY VARIANT

Let us go to the woods,
says this little pig.
What to do there?
says that little pig.

To look for our mother,
says this little pig.
What to do with her?
says that little pig.

To kiss her all over,
says wee little pig.

To play: Touch or hold on to the child's toes in succession, starting with the big toe. When you come to the kissing part, kiss the child "all over" indeed.

HARRY WHISTLE

Another toe-counting game, this one has some Scandinavian connections, as the word oker *(in Icelandic* akr, *in Danish* ager, *and Swedish* aker *but pronounced "oker") means field, as in a field flower.*

Harry Whistle,

Tommy Thistle,

Harry Whibble,

Tommy Thibble,

And little oker-bell.

To play: Again, the toes are touched in turn, though this rhyme has no tickle at the end.

SHOE THE HORSE

This foot rhyme can be very soothing. It also has some Scandinavian counterparts. There is a wilder game for older children called "Shoe the Wild Horse" that was popular at Christmas in the seventeenth century.

Shoe the horse,

Shoe the mare,

Let the little colt go bare.

To play: Pat or smooth the bottom of a child's bare foot for the first two lines and then tap the top lightly for the rest.

WHERE IS THUMBKIN?

This singing game is an American version of a very old English rhyme.

With growing enjoyment

Where is Thumb - kin? Where is Thumb - kin?

Here I am. Here I am. How are you to - day, sir?

Ver -y well, I thank you. Run and hide. Run and hide.

Where is Pointer? etc.

Where is Longman? etc.

Where is Ringman? etc.

Where is Pinkie? etc.

To play: When the question "Where is ...?" is asked, each finger on each hand bobs, one after the other.
On the "How are you ..." the finger describes a circle, one after the other, as if holding a conversation.
And when the instruction about running and hiding is sung, the hands disappear behind the back.

Two Fat Gentlemen

This finger rhyme was popular in Scotland for well over one hundred and fifty years.

Two fat gentlemen
Met in a glen.
Bowed most politely,
Bowed once again.
How do you do? How do you do?
How do you do again?

Two thin ladies
Met in a glen.
Bowed most politely,
Bowed once again.
How do you do? How do you do?
How do you do again?

Two tall policemen
Met in a glen.
Bowed most politely,
Bowed once again.
How do you do? How do you do?
How do you do again?

Two happy schoolboys

Met in a glen.

Bowed most politely,

Bowed once again.

How do you do? How do you do?

How do you do again?

Two little babies

Met in a glen.

Bowed most politely,

Bowed once again.

How do you do? How do you do?

How do you do again?

OTHER NAMES FOR THE FINGERS

Tom Thumbkin,
Bill Wilkins,
Long Daniel,
Bessy Bobtail,
And little Dick.
— *Yorkshire, England*

Tommeltot,
Slickkepot,
Langemand,
Guldbrand,
Lille Peer Spilleman
(Little Peter the Fiddler).
— *Denmark*

And this slightly more complete rhyme:
Thumbkin, Thumbkin
   broke the barn,
Pinikin, Pinikin stole the corn,
Long back'd Gray carried it away.
Old Mid-man sat and saw,
But Peesy-Weesy paid for a'.
— *Scotland*

INCEY WINCEY SPIDER

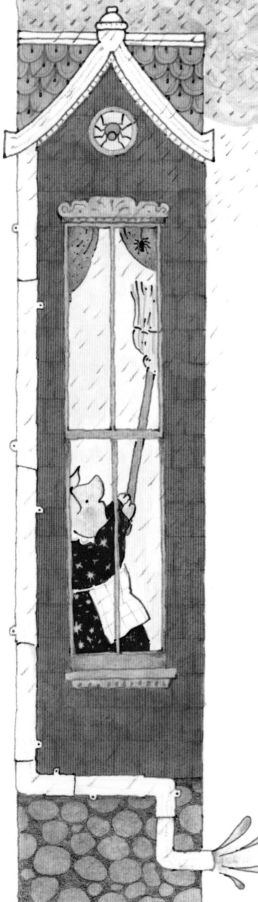

This is probably the best known finger game of all. There have even been award-winning children's picture books made from the text.

Incey wincey spider

Climbed up the water spout.

Down came the rain

And washed poor spider out.

Out came the sunshine

And dried up all the rain,

So incey wincey spider

Climbed up the spout again.

Again!

Sweetly

In-cey win-cey spi-der Climbed up the wa-ter spout.

Down came the rain___ And washed poor spi-der out.

Out came the sun-shine And dried up all the rain, So

in-cey win-cey spi-der Climbed up the spout a-gain.___

To play: Right thumb on left forefinger, then left thumb on right forefinger, you make a walking motion upwards, which the child can imitate. Hands move up and down for the rain. A side-to-side motion indicates the spider being washed out. A large circle with your arms for the rising sun. Then start again. I even shout "Again!" at the end with my grandchildren.

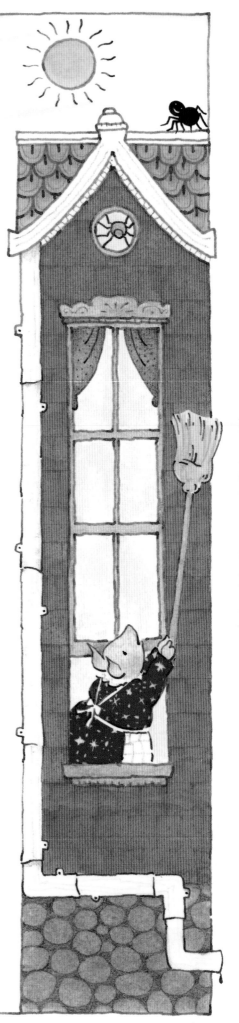

Foxy's Den

A popular British finger-and-fist game.

Put your finger in Foxy's den.

Foxy's not at home.

Foxy's at the back door,

Picking on a bone!

**To play: Make a loose fist. Hold it up with the thumb resting on top.
The child puts a finger in the hole. Catch the finger and hold it tight.**

The Quiet Mouse

An American finger-and-fist game.

Once there lived a quiet mouse.

He lived inside a quiet house.

When all was quiet as could be…

OUT POPPED HE!

**To play: The child puts a finger in the hole in your
fist and pops it out when the verse demands.**

IN WENT THE PRAIRIE DOG

Another finger-and-fist game, popular in America.

In went the prairie dog,

With a little squeal.

Out came the prairie dog,

Looking for a meal.

In went the prairie dog,

Looking for a friend.

Out came the prairie dog

Again.

And AGAIN!

To play: The child puts a finger in your fist and takes it out again as the verse demands.

HICKORY, DICKORY DOCK

First published as a limerick in Tom Thumb's Pretty Song Book
in 1744, it gained a tune about a century later.

To play: Walk up the child's arm with your first two fingers. At the line "The clock struck one",
give the child a nose kiss. Then have the fingers run back down again.

DICKERY, DICKERY

This verse is closely related to the song,
but there's more to play with in it.

Dickery, dickery dock,
The mouse ran up the clock.
The clock struck one,
The mouse ran down,
Dickery, dickery dock.

Dickery, dickery dock.
The mouse ran up the clock.
The clock struck trey,
Mouse ran away,
Dickery, dickery dock.

Dickery, dickery dock,
The mouse ran up the clock.
The clock struck ten,
Mouse came again,
Dickery, dickery dock.

To play: Just add on to the gestures of "Hickory, Dickory Dock".

HERE IS THE CHURCH

This little ditty is extremely popular throughout the English-speaking world.

Here is the church,

and here is the steeple.

Open the doors,

and see all the people.

Here is the parson

going upstairs,

And here he is a-saying

his prayers!

To play: Lock your fingers knuckle to knuckle. That is the church. Put your little fingers up and lean one on the other. That is the steeple. Swing your thumbs open – the church doors. Waggle your fingers – all the people. Pick your fingers apart one at a time – the stairs. Hands together – saying prayers.

48

KNIVES AND FORKS

If you can play "Here Is the Church", you can play this fingers game.

Here are my lady's knives and forks.

Here is my lady's table.

Here is my lady's looking glass,

And here is the baby's cradle.

To play: Lock your fingers knuckle to knuckle. Invert so that the fingers now point up – knives and forks. Invert again so knuckles are up – the table. Face knuckles towards you – the looking glass. Knuckles down, rocking – the baby's cradle.

BO PEEPER

This face-tapping rhyme comes in many variations.

Bo peeper,

Nose dreeper,

Chin chopper,

White lopper,

Red rag,

And little gap.

To play: At each line, you touch the baby's face successively for eye, nose, chin, tooth, tongue and mouth.

BROW BRINKY

Another face-tapping rhyme.

Brow brinky,

Eye winky,

Chin choppy,

Nose noppy,

Cheek cherry,

Mouth merry.

To play: At each line, touch the baby's face successively for forehead, eye, chin, nose, cheek, mouth.

BROW BENDER

The opening four lines of this verse were first printed in Tommy Thumb's Song Book *in 1788.*

Brow bender,

Eye peeper,

Nose dropper,

Mouth eater,

Chin chopper,

Knock at the door,

Ring the bell,

Lift up the latch,

Walk in,

Take a chair,

Sit by there,

And how do you do this morning?

**To play: Touch the named features one at a time: forehead, eyes, nose, mouth, chin. At
"Knock at the door", tickle the child's chin. At "Ring the bell", lightly pull the child's ear. At
"Lift the latch", raise the child's nose slightly and then pop your finger into the child's mouth.**

Here Sits the Lord Mayor

A face-tapping rhyme with a bit more to it.

Here sits the lord mayor.

Here sit his men.

Here sits the cockadoodle.

Here sits the hen.

Here sit the little chickens.

Here they run in.

Chin chopper! Chin chopper!

Chin chopper, chin!

To play: At each line, touch the baby's face for each feature mentioned. In order, these are: the forehead, the eyes, the right cheek, the left cheek, the nose, the mouth and the chin.

CHOP-A-NOSE DAY

A face-tapper with a giggle at the end.

My mother and your mother

Went over the way.

Said my mother to your mother,

It's chop-a-nose day!

To play: Slide your fingers down the child's face from forehead to nose, at which point you pinch the nose
lightly and hold up your thumb between the second and third finger as if you have taken off the nose!

53

ROUND ABOUT

A palm tickling game.

Round about, round about,

Runs the little hare.

First it runs that way,

Then it runs up THERE!

(under the arm)

COWS AND HORSES

A nineteenth century hand game.

Cows and horses walk on four legs,

Little children walk on two legs.

Fishes swim in water clear,

Birds fly up into the air.

One, two, three, four, five,

Catching fishes all alive.

Why did you let them go?

Because they bit my fingers so.

Which finger did they bite?

The little finger on the right.

To play: Using two fingers on each hand, mimic prancing cows and horses. Then use one finger per hand for the children. Wave hands horizontally for the fish, flap hands for birds, clap hands for the counting, mime catching fish with hands, then let the fish go. The adult asks the question and the child answers. Then hold up the little finger on the right hand.

TICKLE YE

A tickling rhyme that seems to be used for telling the future.

Tickle ye, tickle ye in the hand.

If you laugh, you are a man.

If you cry, you are a baby,

If you dance, you are a lady,

If you hiccup, you'll be a lord

And health and wealth be your reward.

Tickle ye, tickle ye on the knee.

If you laugh, a farmer you'll be,

If you cry, you'll be a writer,

If you hit, you'll be a fighter,

If you call, an actor you'll be

And health and wealth will follow thee.

A GOOD CHILD

Another tickle game.

A good child, a good child,

As I suppose you be,

You'll neither laugh nor smile

At the tickling of…your KNEE!

Clap, Clap,

Clap

Pat-a-cakes are small buns with currants. The song was first printed in 1698.

Sprightly

Pat - a - cake, pat - a - cake, ba - ker's man,

Make me a cake as fast as you can. Pat it and prick it and

mark it with a *B*, And put it in the o - ven for Ba - by and me.

To play: The child sits facing you. Clap your hands together, then clap the child's hands alternately for the first four lines. Next mime rolling dough balls, marking them with a *B* (or even the initial of your own child's name). Turn your hands over and with palms upwards, gently poke your child's tummy, as if putting dough in the oven.**

PAT-A-CAKE
Around the World

Bake, bake a cake,
Hear the baker call.
He who wants to bake a cake
Has seven things in all:
Eggs and salt,
Milk and flour,
Butter and lard,
And saffron to make it all yellow.
—*Germany (Backe, backe Kuchen…)*

Little cakes and more little cakes,
For Mother, the prettiest.
Round loaves and more round loaves,
For the littlest baby (boy or girl)
And for father the big lumps.
—*Spain (Tortitas y más tortitas…)*

Hand, little hand, hand, little hand,
Bread and figs for the lady,
Here comes Papa, bringing us candy,
But none for the little baby.
—*Italy (Mano, manuzzi…)*

**To play: Fit actions to the words
after four lines of hand-clapping.**

PEASE PORRIDGE HOT

This clapping rhyme was first printed in The Newest Christmas Box *in 1797.*
Children used to clap their hands warm on cold days. Pease porridge is a thin pudding made of boiled split peas.

Pease porridge hot,

Pease porridge cold,

Pease porridge in the pot,

Nine days old.

Some like it hot.

Some like it cold.

Some like it in the pot

Nine days old.

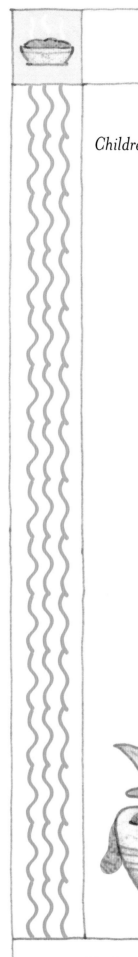

To play: Alternate hand-clapping between your own hands (twice), your knees, repeat; then your hands together,
right hand to the child's right hand, hands together, then your left hand to the child's. End with three claps together.

Pease Porridge in America

The English colonists brought "Pease Porridge Hot" to America, where it took on a political aspect.

Slap hands, slap,
Fall tyrants, fall,
These are the days of Liberty,
One and all.

To play: Modify instructions on the previous page.

Pease Porridge in the City

Found all over the world, this is another game played the same way and with the same rhythm as "Pease Porridge Hot".

Oh sir, oh sir,
Where should I go, sir,
For a loaf of bread, sir?
Go to the grocer.

Yes sir, yes sir,
That's where I'll go, sir,
For a loaf of bread, sir,
Straight to the grocer.

Oh sir, oh sir,
Where should I go, sir,
For a polar bear, sir,
Straight to the grocer?

No sir, no sir,
Not to the grocer,
For a polar bear, sir,
Go to the zoo, sir.

Yes sir, yes sir,
That's where I'd go, sir,
For a polar bear, sir,
Straight to the zoo, sir.

CLAP HANDS, CLAP HANDS

Hand-clapping games like this were very popular in the nineteenth century and are still played today. This nursery rhyme was used for hand clapping.

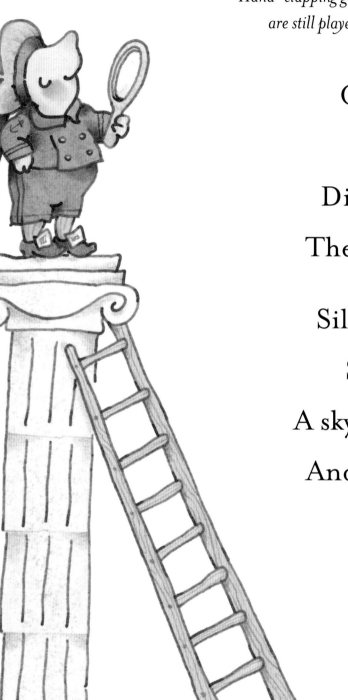

Clap hands, clap hands,

Hie Tommy Randy,

Did you see my good man?

They call him Cock-a-bandy.

Silken stockings on his legs,

Silver buckles glancin',

A sky-blue bonnet on his head.

And oh! But he is handsome.

**To play: Clap your own hands; then clap the child's two hands; repeat. Clap your own hands, then your knees twice.
Clap hands, clap right to right hand with child, clap hands, then left to left. Clap hands, then knees twice.**

A Variety of Hand Claps

Clap hands, clap hands,
Dishes in a battle,
Pots and pans all crash about.
Bang! Rattle! Rattle!
—*New York, USA*

The woods are dark,
The grass is green.
Here comes Sally with a tambourine.
A tambourine, a tambourine,
Here comes Sally with a tambourine.
—*Worcester, England*

John, John, where have you been
All this live-long day?
Down in the alley,
courting Sally,
Picking up cinders,
breaking windows,
Feeding monkeys,
riding donkeys,
Chasing bulldogs,
All this live-long day.
—*Australia*

MISS MARY MACK

This American hand-clap song, based on a Shropshire skipping game,
was first recorded amongst Irish immigrant children in Boston in 1865.

She asked her mother, mother, mother,

For fifty cents, cents, cents,

To watch the elephant, elephant, elephant,

Jump over the fence, fence, fence

He jumped so high, high, high,

He reached the sky, sky, sky,

And he never came back, back, back

Till the fourth of July, July, July.

To play: There are so many variations of the hand-clapping, you can even make up your own.

MARY MACK
Around the World

Mary Mack is dressed in black,
Silver buttons down her back,
Walking on the railroad track.
—*Boston, USA 1865*

Betsy Blue came all in black,
Silver buttons down her back,
Every button cost a crown,
Every lady turn around.
Alligoshi, alligoshee,
Turn the bridle over my knee.
—*Shropshire, England*

Mary Mack, dressed in black,
Three gold buttons down her back.
I love coffee, I love tea,
I love the boys,
And the boys love me.
—*St. Louis, USA 1895*

Miss Mary Mack,
Dressed in black,
Silver buttons down her back.
I love coffee, I love tea,
I love boys,
And the boys love me.
—*Pennsylvania, USA 1888*

HAVE YOU EVER, EVER, EVER

This hand-clap song originated in America and is now popular in Britain.

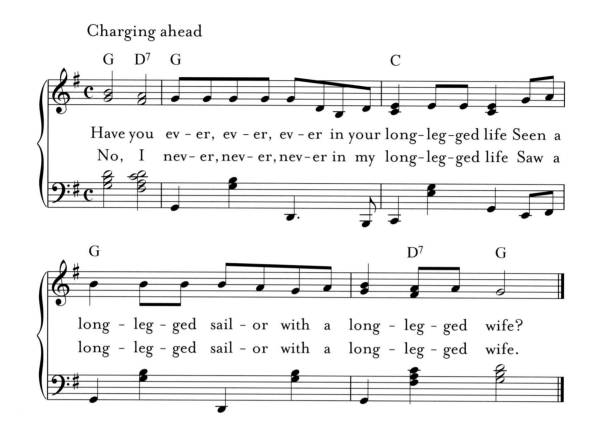

Have you ever, ever, ever in your knock-kneed life, etc.

Have you ever, ever, ever in your bow-legged life, etc.

Have you ever, ever, ever in your pigeon-toed life, etc.

Have you ever, ever, ever in your duck-toed life, etc.

**To play: Hands begin on knees. Clap together, right hands, clap together, left hands. Clap together.
Then strike both hands with child twice. Begin again, getting faster and faster as you go along.**

A Sailor Went to Sea

A popular singsong game that started in the nursery, moved to the playground,
and eventually ended up in a Fred Astaire film.

A sailor went to chop, chop, chop, etc.

A sailor went to knee, knee, knee, etc.

A sailor went to toe, toe, toe, etc.

To play: Clap on lap, then hands together. Act out the words: "to sea" by saluting the child; "to see", hand over eye; "the bottom", hands pointing down; "to chop", chop one hand into the angle of the other elbow; "to knee", touch the child's knee; etc.

Take a Bow

I'm a Little Teapot

This popular action-rhyme originated from America.

Rocking gently

I'm a lit-tle tea-pot, short and stout. Here's my han-dle, here's my spout. When I see the tea-cups hear me shout: "Tip me up and pour me out!"

I'm a special teapot, it is true.

Here, let me show you what I can do.

I can change my handle and my spout.

Tip me up and pour me out.

To play: This is an action rhyme, the child following the adult's lead. Sit or stand straight for the first line. Place your left hand on your hip for the handle, and extend your right arm — bent at the wrist and elbow — upwards for the spout. Getting "steamed up" means getting excited, so excitement should show in your face. Then at the "tip me over and pour me out" line, bend over at the waist towards the extended arm, as if pouring tea out of the spout. For the second verse, simply follow the words.

DOWN BY THE STATION

Popular in schools and nurseries, this American song has been around for at least fifty years.

With spirit

Down by the sta-tion ear-ly in the morn-ing, See the lit-tle puf-fer-trains all in a row. See the en-gine dri-ver pull the lit-tle han-dle. Toot! Toot! Puff! Puff! Off we go.

To play: On the first line, move your hands, turned palms down, up and down rhythmically. On the word "See", bring your right hand up to shade your eyes, and move your head from side to side as if viewing the scene. The engine driver pulling the handle is mimed in rhythm. At the words "Off we go", wave goodbye.

INDEX OF FIRST LINES

INDEX OF FIRST LINES (continued)

Abrahams, Roger D., and Lois Rankin. *Counting-Out Rhymes.* Austin: University of Texas Press, 1980.

Baring-Gould, William S., and Ceil Baring-Gould. *The Annotated Mother Goose.* New York: Bramhall House, n.d.

Cole, Joanna, and Stephanie Calmenson. *The Eentsy Weentsy Spider: Fingerplays and Action Rhymes.* New York: Mulberry/William Morrow, 1991.

Glazer, Tom. *Eye Winker, Tom Tinker, Chin Chopper: Fifty Musical Fingerplays.* New York: Doubleday, 1973.

Green, Percy B. *A History of Nursery Rhymes.* London: Greening & Co., 1899.

Opie, Iona and Peter. *The Singing Game.* New York: Oxford University Press, 1985.

Poulsson, Emilie. *Fingerplays for Nursery and Kindergarten.* New York: Dover Publications, 1971; reprint of Boston: D. Lothrop Company, 1893.

Seeger, Ruth Crawford. *American Folk Songs for Children.* New York: Doubleday, 1948.

Vinton, Iris. *The Folkways Omnibus of Children's Games.* Harrisburg, Penn.: Stackpole Books, 1970.

Wessells, Katharine Tyler. *The Golden Song Book.* New York: Simon and Schuster, 1945.

Wilner, Isabel, and Sam Williams. *The Baby's Game Book.* New York: Greenwillow, 2000.

Yolen, Jane, and Adam Stemple. *The Lap-Time Song and Play Book.* San Diego: Harcourt Brace, 1989.

About the Editor, Illustrator and Arranger

JANE YOLEN has played many of these games with her three children and six grandchildren. The author of more than 250 books for children and young adults, including the Caldecott-winning *Owl Moon* and the *New York Times* best-selling *How Do Dinosaurs Say Good Night?* and its sequels, she is an oral storyteller as well. With her husband, she lives half the year in Massachusetts, USA, and half the year in Scotland.

WILL HILLENBRAND is the acclaimed illustrator of *Kiss the Cow!* by Phyllis Root, *The Biggest, Best Snowman* and *Please Say Please* by Margery Cuyler, and the author-illustrator of *Down by the Station*. He lives in Ohio, USA, with his wife and son who inspire much of his work.

ADAM STEMPLE is a full-time musician and author who has published more than a dozen music books. He lives in Minneapolis with his wife, two children and a fish.